for Rae, Rowan,
Michelle & Alvin.
and a
special Thankyou
to Pauliina for the idea.

Illustrations copyright © 2003 by Jane Cabrera

First published in the United Kingdom in 2003

by Gullane Children's Books, an imprint of Pinwheel Ltd., Winchester House,

259-269 Old Marylebone Road. London NW15XJ, United Kingdom.

First published in the United States of America by Holiday House, Inc. in 2005. All Rights Reserved

Printed in China www.holidayhouse.com

Library of Congress Cataloging-in-Publication Data First Edition 1 3 5 7 9 10 8 6 4 2

Cabrera, Jane. If you're happy and you know it /

Jane Cabrera.—1st ed. p. cm.

Summary: An elephant, a monkey, and a giraffe join other animals

everyone to express their happiness through voice and movement. to sing different verses of this popular song that encourages

1. Children's songs, English—Texts.

2. Animals—Songs and music. 3. Singing games. 4. Games. 5. Songs.] ISBN 0-8234-1881-2 (hardcover)

[1. Happiness—Songs and music.

I. Titles: If you're happy and you know it. II. Title.

PZ8.3.C12211f2005   782.42164'0268—dc22   [E] 2004047264

If You're Happy and You Know It!

Jane Cabrera

Holiday House / New York

Are you feeling happy today?
Join me and my friends
for some sing-along fun. . . .

If you're happy and you know it,
CLAP your hands
If you're happy and you know it,
CLAP your hands
If you're happy and you know it,
And you really want to show it

If you're happy and you know it,
CLAP YOUR HANDS!

If you're happy and you know it,
STAMP your feet

If you're happy and you know it,
STAMP your feet

If you're happy and you know it,
And you really want to show it

If you're happy and you know it,
STAMP YOUR FEET!

If you're happy and you know it,
NOD your head
If you're happy and you know it,
NOD your head
If you're happy and you know it,
And you really want to show it

If you're happy and you know it,
NOD YOUR HEAD!

If you're happy and you know it,
  ROAR out loud
If you're happy and you know it,
  ROAR out loud
If you're happy and you know it,
And you really want to show it

If you're happy and you know it,

ROAR
OUT LOUD!

If you're happy and you know it,
SPIN AROUND
If you're happy and you know it,
SPIN AROUND
If you're happy and you know it,
And you really want to show it

If you're happy
and you know it,
SPIN AROUND!

If you're happy and you know it,
go KISS KISS
If you're happy and you know it,
go KISS KISS
If you're happy and you know it,
And you really want to show it

If you're happy and you know it,
go KISS KISS!

If you're happy and you know it, FLAP your arms
If you're happy and you know it, FLAP your arms
If you're happy and you know it,

And you really want to show it
If you're happy and you know it,
FLAP YOUR ARMS!

If you're happy and you know it,
   say SQUEAK SQUEAK
If you're happy and you know it,
   say SQUEAK SQUEAK
If you're happy and you know it,
And you really want to show it

If you're happy and you know it, say SQUEAK SQUEAK!

If you're happy and you know it, JUMP AROUND!
If you're happy and you know it, JUMP AROUND!
If you're happy and you know it,
And you really want to show it

If you're happy and you know it,
JUMP AROUND!

If you're happy and you know it,
And you really want to show it
If you're happy and you know it,

SHOUT...

We are!